A FAMILY JOURNEY

A Candlelight Celebration
For Advent And Christmas Eve

Dallas A. Brauninger

CSS Publishing Company, Inc.
Lima, Ohio

A FAMILY JOURNEY

Copyright 1994
The CSS Publishing Company, Inc.
Lima, Ohio

All rights reserved. No part of this publication may be reproduced, stored in a retrieval system, or transmitted in any form or by any means, electronic, mechanical, photocopying, recording, or otherwise, without the prior permission of the publisher. Inquiries should be addressed to: The CSS Publishing Company, Inc., 517 South Main Street, P.O. Box 4503, Lima, Ohio 45802-4503.

ISBN 0-7880-0099-3   PRINTED IN U.S.A.

*Dedicated to
our Church Family*

Table Of Contents

Introduction To The Services	7
Advent 1	9
Advent 2	11
Advent 3	14
Advent 4	16
Christmas Eve	18
Complete Order Of Worship	20
Banner	22

Introduction To The Services

These services for the lighting of the candles of the wreath during Advent and on Christmas Eve are designed with the entire family in mind, both as hearers and as participants, and with a full understanding of the meaning of family.

Each week a different family will enter the chancel to light the Advent candles. Worship planners are encouraged to select families of a variety of type and age. Congregations can then affirm a single-parent family or a couple without children or whose children are grown as well as traditional two-parent, two-children families. Even a family of one may be thought of as a family unit because that person is part of the extended church family. The member(s) of the family will read the reflection, light the Advent candle(s) and place the symbol and word on the expanding banner, which has been prepared by other members of the church family.

On Christmas Eve, a family with a newborn infant, along with other siblings, will come to the chancel at the specified time. Dressed in today's clothing, they will place their baby on a blanket in the hay-filled manger and stay by the baby as the children of the church gather around.

A centering comment is provided at the beginning of the bulletin to assist worshipers in focusing on the theme for each service. This is for personal meditation before worship begins.[1]

Scripture readings will be read from the lectern by older youths or members of the youth group. Youths will want to practice reading with the microphone.

Invite the children of the church to sit on the chancel steps or where they usually sit for the children's sermon so they can see what is happening. The storyteller, who should be the same person each time, should sit facing the children and address them as is the custom at their usual children's time. The storyteller may want to be dressed in the robe, sandals and head covering of an adult in the days of Jesus.

Following the weekly addition to the banner, the congregation will share a unison prayer response and the singing of one verse of

"Mary and Joseph in Bethlehem Town."[2] On Christmas Eve, the congregation will sing verse one as the children sit around the manger. After the congregational response, they will sing the remaining three verses.

Alternatively, these services, including the banner making, may be combined as a single Christmas Eve celebration. A complete Order of Worship follows the individual presentations in this book.

---

[1] From Brauninger's *Centering Toward A Deeper Spirituality*, a resource book of sentence prayer starters. Available from the author.

[2] Written in 1978, this hymn "is to be sung with a sense of joyous movement," writes its creator in *God's Glory: Hymns by Dosia Carlson* (555 W. Glendale Avenue, Phoenix, AZ 85021, 602-274-5022). "The strong 2-beat rhythm suggests a steadily rocking cradle. Singers should strongly affirm that last statement of each verse, 'Christ is born.' "

Advent 1

Bulletin Meditation Note
Focus: Symbols — Conception and Star
Consider this sign: From unknown spaces comes the meeting of two possibilities. Within its miracle the new begins. A guiding star lights the pathway, then and now.

Scripture Reading:

Reader 1:
Therefore the Lord himself will give you a sign. Look, the young woman is with child and shall bear a son, and shall name him Immanuel. (Isaiah 7:14 NRSV)

Reader 2:
...an angel of the Lord appeared to [Joseph] in a dream and said, "Joseph, son of David, do not be afraid to take Mary as your wife, for the child conceived in her is from the Holy Spirit." (Matthew 1:20 NRSV)

(Invite the children of the church to sit on the chancel steps where they can see what is happening.)

Storyteller Addresses Children:
All babies are special, aren't they? One night, God came to Mary as an angel in a dream. God told Mary she was going to have a baby. Mary was surprised. That's how God had decided to come on earth. Can you imagine how you would feel if God had chosen you? Surprised? A little scared? Close to God? Very special? That's how Mary felt, too.

Soon after that, God also came to Joseph in a dream. God told Joseph about the baby growing inside Mary's womb. I wonder how Joseph felt. He loved Mary very much and knew God wanted him to take care of her. In the same dream, God told Joseph to name the baby Jesus, who is also called Immanuel which means God is with us.

Lighting The First Candle On The Advent Wreath

Reflection:

The Bethlehem star must have been *some* star. We can only imagine the path a full moon cuts across an open pasture. If we turn and walk away from the light, we block its light with the shadow of our own body. If we follow the path of light, the darkness on either side appears to fall away. To observers, we appear covered with light. We seem to become part of the light, absorbing it as we walk toward it.

The path shown by the Bethlehem star is that kind of light, showing clearly the way to the manger. We hear no stories of hesitation. The shepherds simply follow. Curiosity? Faith? Quiet searching? We don't know what went on in their hearts, but the family of God followed the light.

Securing The Star And The First Word To The Banner

Congregational Prayer Response:

God of the Christmas star, we know your light is so strong it cannot be put out by any darkness. Awaken our wanting to see the star. Help us to meet each day believing this truth. Unglue the stuck feet of our hearts so we can follow its light. Help us be sharers of the light and not blockers of its path. Amen.

Hymn: *Mary And Joseph In Bethlehem Town (Verse 1)*

Advent 2

Bulletin Meditation Note
*Focus: Symbol — The Highway through the Desert
Consider this sign: Into the desert of our life a highway of purpose shows itself.*

Scripture Reading:

Reader 1:
A voice cries out: "In the wilderness prepare the way of the Lord, make straight in the desert a highway for our God." (Isaiah 40:3 NRSV)

Reader 2:
In those days a decree went out from Emperor Augustus that all the world should be registered. This was the first registration and was taken while Quirinius was governor of Syria. All went to their own towns to be registered. Joseph also went from the town of Nazareth in Galilee to Judea, to the city of David called Bethlehem, because he was descended from the house and family of David. He went to be registered with Mary, to whom he was engaged and who was expecting a child. (Luke 2:1-5)

(Invite the children of the church to sit on the chancel steps.)

Storyteller Addresses Children:
Mary and Joseph were excited as they waited for their unusual baby to be born. Sometimes Mary told Joseph to put his hand over her tummy to feel the happy baby move around inside her. Joseph loved feeling the baby kick. He could hardly wait to hold Jesus in his arms and tell him how much he loved him.

Joseph and Mary hoped Jesus would be born before they had to make the trip to Judea to Joseph's hometown of Bethlehem. But it didn't work out that way. Today when it's time for the census, a piece of paper to fill out comes in the mail. Back then, every man and his family had to return to the place where the man was born.

So Joseph and Mary left their home in Nazareth in Galilee to register himself with Mary. If we drove from Nazareth to Bethlehem today, it wouldn't take more than about an hour and a half. Back then, people didn't have cars. They had to walk the 70 miles.

The trip took Mary and Joseph a few days — even with the donkey that carried their supplies. Look at all the other people following the road up to Bethlehem. "Look, Mary, there's Stephen and Salome and their boys."

Mary and Joseph waved to friends along the way who were also going to Bethlehem. There wasn't time to stop and talk but sometimes they walked together for awhile with people they knew. The road sure was crowded with people and with donkey droppings.

Lighting The Second Candle On The Advent Wreath

Reflection:

The symbol of the path is rich with images. Take one and follow it where it leads you:

A way through the confusion and chaos life brings.

The abrupt change a new superhighway brings as it cuts a concrete swath through a farmer's bean field.

A sense of direction and meaning.

The particular signs marking the route a Christian chooses.

A return to a childhood foot trail and finding the path needs to be cleared.

The finding of a road after you wandered lost.

The road to Bethlehem, the road to Jerusalem, the road to Golgotha.

Creating a path of love, strength and integrity for your family because of your nurture.

Cutting a path of hope through a wilderness of despair, a path of caring where there is none, a path of justice.

Clearing a way through the business of your life to make room for Christmas.

Securing The Path And The Second Word To The Banner

Congregational Prayer Response:
Set our feet on your path, God. Amen.

Hymn: *Mary And Joseph In Bethlehem Town (Verse 1)*

Advent 3

Bulletin Meditation Note
Focus: Experience God as opening
Prayer: Opening God, when I have patience and wait, always you bring possibility.

Scripture Reading:

Reader 1:
I am going to send an angel in front of you, to guard you on the way and to bring you to the place that I have prepared. (Exodus 23:20 NRSV)

Reader 2:
I will appoint a place for my people Israel, and will plant them, so that they may live in their own place, and be disturbed no more; and evildoers shall wear them down no more, as they did formerly. (1 Chronicles 17:9 NRSV)

Reader 3:
When they had heard the king, they set out; and there, ahead of them, went the star that they had seen at its rising, until it stopped over the place where the child was. (Matthew 2:9 NRSV)

(Invite the children of the church to sit on the chancel steps.)

Storyteller Addresses Children:
Mary couldn't walk as fast as the others. Joseph took care of Mary. "Mary, the road is getting rough here. I'm going to carry our supplies on my back for awhile. You ride the donkey and take a little rest. Does that help, Mary? We don't have too much farther to go."

"Joseph, I don't think I can make it much farther tonight."

"Okay, Mary, there's a house up here. Let's see if they can put us up for the night.... Well, Mary, I'm sorry that didn't work out."

"But it did help, Joseph, just to stop awhile. Let me walk again.

Our load of belongings is too heavy for you, Joseph."

"I'm okay, Mary. It's beautiful out here, isn't it? When I was a small boy, sometimes at night after my dad and I finished our work in the carpenter shop, we'd walk through the field over to my uncle's herd of sheep. My dad and my uncle would talk late into the night as they protected the sheep. I sat out by the sheepfold and watched the stars. Sometimes one of my uncle's lambs would snuggle in my arms."

Lighting The Third Candle On The Advent Wreath

Reflection:
Soon, Jesus will have a place, a little bed of hay in a stable cave. Soon, with the birth of Jesus, God comes to the place God created.

We are all looking for a place. Some of us have always lived in one house or the same town. That is our place. Some children share two families and two homes. We belong in both places. Some families have moved many times. Each time we say goodbye, we feel sad. For awhile, we hesitate before stretching ourselves to make new friends. Then, we say hello and our smiles return. We have found a new place to call home.

No matter where we find a place, God has been there first to welcome us with God's presence, with possibility. Even at the end of our earthly life, we trust the one who has gone before us to make for us a new place.

Securing The Houses, Stable And Third Word To The Banner

Congregational Prayer Response:
Thank you, God, for being in each place we call home. Amen.

Hymn: *Mary And Joseph In Bethlehem Town (Verse 1)*

Advent 4

Bulletin Meditation Note
Focus: Symbol — Mary and Joseph
Consider these signs: Within each of us is a life-giving nourisher and teacher of trust. Within each of us is the protector and one who leads us out toward discovery of the world.

Scripture Reading:

Reader:
While they were there, the time came for her to deliver her child. And she gave birth to her firstborn son and wrapped him in bands of cloth, and laid him in a manger, because there was no place for them in the inn. (Luke 2:6-7 NRSV)

(Invite the children of the church to sit on the chancel steps.)

Storyteller Addresses Children:
"Joseph," Mary said, "I feel like we've been walking forever. I'm going to have to lie down very soon. I think the baby is going to be born tonight."
"Oh, Mary, we must find you a place to rest. We are so near Bethlehem. See the clump of trees in the distance. There must be an inn up there somewhere."
"God will help us, Joseph."
"Here, Mary. Let's try this house. Please, God, we are very tired. We must find a place for Mary to have her baby."

Lighting The Fourth Candle On The Advent Wreath

Reflection:
God sends special people in our lives to care for us and to look after us. When family members become too old to care for themselves, their grown children take care of their parents or find other caregivers. When family members are too young to care for

themselves, a mother or a father, a grandparent or another person who loves them looks after them.

When we are those who nurture and protect, when we are those who teach what it means to trust, we recognize that every family, however large or small, is a holy family. Every family is part of God's family.

Securing The Family And Fourth Word To The Banner

Congregational Prayer Response:
Thank you, God, for our families. Help us to be loving and kind members of our families. Thank you for sending Mary and Joseph to care for your child, Jesus. Amen.

Hymn: *Mary And Joseph In Bethlehem Town (Verse 1)*

Christmas Eve

Bulletin Meditation Note
Focus: Symbol — The Baby Jesus
Consider this sign: What surprising tomorrows are contained in the most fragile, vulnerable house — the human infant.

Scripture Reading:

Reader 1:
Then he said, "Come no closer! Remove the sandals from your feet, for the place on which you are standing is holy ground." (Exodus 3:5 NRSV)

Reader 2:
"To you is born this day in the city of David a Savior, who is the Messiah, the Lord. This will be a sign for you: you will find a child wrapped in bands of cloth and lying in a manger." (Luke 2:11-12 NRSV)

Readers 1 & 2:
And suddenly there was with the angel a multitude of the heavenly host, praising God and saying, "Glory to God in the highest heaven, and on earth peace among those whom he favors!" (Luke 2:13-14 NRSV)

(Invite a family with an infant to come to the chancel, placing the child in the manger as the organist plays softly the hymn "Mary And Joseph in Bethlehem Town." Ask the children of the church to gather around the manger.)

Hymn: *Mary And Joseph In Bethlehem Town (Verse 1)*
(Children sit on the floor around the manger.)

Lighting All Candles On The Advent Wreath
Plus The Christ Candle

Reflection:
It is on this night of the holy birth that we all come to the manger. We feel the change come over us, erasing the distance of time and space. The holy birth is present in each birth. The same first-time parents are present at each first birth. The same depth of wonder and love and hope for new beginnings is present in each of us as we come to the manger.

God chose to come to us as a baby in a manger in a stable. The breath of the animals warms the air. The cave stable is private and quiet. Fresh hay cushions the manger. Love surrounds the baby.

Receive this newborn. Lift this baby out of the manger and into your own cradling arms. Gently, humbly, in a manger, you come to us, God.

Securing The Manger With Baby And The Fifth Word To The Banner

Congregational Prayer Response:
    Don't Keep Me In A Manger[3]

    Don't keep me in a manger;
    My coming's more than a lullaby.
    Lift me out with your arms;
    Let me grow.

    Don't keep me in a manger
    Back then.
    Take me where I'll make a difference
    Now
    With you.

Hymn: *"Mary And Joseph In Bethlehem Town" (Verses 2, 3 and 4) (All participants return to their seats during the singing of the hymn.)*

---

[3]Copyright by the writer and first published in Jan-Feb. 1993 issue of *These Days*.

Order Of Worship
A Family Journey Christmas Eve Service

Scripture Reading: Isaiah 7:14; Matthew 1:20
Optional Storytelling
Lighting Of First Candle
    Placement Of Star + STAR On Banner
Reflection
Congregational Prayer Response
Hymn: *Mary And Joseph In Bethlehem Town (v. 1)*
Scripture Reading: Isaiah 40:3; Luke 2:1-5
Optional Storytelling
Lighting Of Second Candle
    Placement Of Path + PATH On Banner
Reflection
Congregation Prayer Response
Hymn: *Mary And Joseph In Bethlehem Town (v. 2)*
Scripture Reading: Exodus 23:20; 1 Chronicles 17:9; Matthew 2:9
Optional Storytelling
Lighting Of Third Candle
    Placement Of Buildings + PLACE On Banner
Reflection
Congregational Prayer Response
Hymn: *Mary And Joseph In Bethlehem Town (v. 3)*
Scripture Reading: Luke 2:6-7
Optional Storytelling

Lighting Of Fourth Candle
    Placement Of Mary And Joseph + FAMILY On Banner
Reflection
Congregational Prayer Response
Hymn: *Mary And Joseph In Bethlehem Town (v. 4)*
Scripture Reading: Exodus 3:5; Luke 2:11-14
Holy Family And Children Of The Church To The Manger
Lighting Of Christ Candle
    Placement Of Manger And Jesus + BABY On Banner
Reflection
Congregational Response
Hymn: *Mary And Joseph In Bethlehem Town (v. 1)*

Banner

Dimensions Of Banner: 36" x 62-1/2"
Primary rectangle: (36" x 46")
Bottom triangles: (7" at top, 9-1/8" length of sides from top edge to bottom point which is 8-1/2" from 3-1/2" center of top)
Yarn tassels (8")

Materials:
- natural color burlap
- unbleached muslin backing
- 36" strip of dark blue quilted material cut on top suggests hills OR machine quilt dark blue calico over slight padding for hills
- several colors of felt scraps for free-form buildings plus backing
- dark brown felt for stable, winding path and triangles
- white felt OR bright liquid paintstitching for lettering
- dots of black loop and hook for symbols
- 36" strip of black loop and hook for felt triangles
- white or dark brown yarn for full tassels
- 6" x 3" cardboard for shaping tassels
- dark brown macrame or braided yarn for hanging
- 2 yardsticks to weight top and bottom
- optional 1" stencils to fit lettering
- fabric glue for felt words on felt triangles

Notes To Banner Committee:
After sewing quilted hills to burlap, right sides together, stitch muslin backing to burlap 1/2" from edge at top and sides, leaving insert slits for yardsticks. Machine stitch strip of loop and hook 1" from bottom across banner. Trim corners. Turn envelope right side out. Press flat. Machine stitch width of yardstick plus 1/4 inch across top and bottom to encase yardstick. Slip in yardsticks and attach hanging yarn. Cut 5 felt triangles and affix fastening strip of loop and hook to backs. Glue or paint on words. Affix loops and hooks on banner as needed each week.

Construct free-form felt buildings as one panel with frame of stable larger so it will stand out as well as hold felt silhouettes of Mary and Joseph.

Optional: Stable frame may be cut from dark brown calico over slight padding.

Prepare Symbols And Word Triangles For Placement:
Advent 1   star + STAR
Advent 2   path + PATH
Advent 3   buildings, stable + PLACE
Advent 4   Mary and Joseph + FAMILY
Christmas Eve   Manger with Jesus + BABY

36"

48"

natural burlap backing

shiny fabric ←

Quilted hills (Dk. Blue)

bright roofs, windows, doors on orange, green, brown buildings

(white)   (Dk. Brown)

(grazing sheep in field)

(Dark Green or Brown Path)

STAR   PATH   PLACE   FAMILY   BABY